HOW TO DRAW HOLIDAY PICTURES

Barbara Soloff Levy

DOVER PUBLICATIONS, INC.
Mineola, New York

Note

All over the world, people look forward to celebrating holidays. In this delightful book, you will learn to draw pictures for many different holidays. Most of the holidays in this book fall on the same date each year, but some do not, such as Easter, Jewish New Year, Eid-al-Fitr, and Thanksgiving.

There are several steps to each drawing. Start with the simplest step (number 1). Then do the next steps in number order—most drawings have four steps, but a few have two or three. You may want to trace the steps first, just to get a feel for drawing. Use a pencil in case you need to make changes along the way. Erase the dotted lines when you get to the last step.

When you are pleased with your drawing, you can go over the lines with a felt-tip pen or colored pencil. Finally, you can color in your drawings any way you wish. After you have finished all thirty drawings, why don't you try to make up some drawings of your own? You can use the holidays in this book, for a start.

Have fun!

Bibliographical Note

How to Draw Holiday Pictures is a new work, first published by Dover Publications, Inc., in 2007.

International Standard Book Number: 0-486-45662-5

Manufactured in the United States of America
Dover Publications, Inc., 31 East 2nd Street, Mineola, N.Y. 11501

1
2
3
4

1
2
3
4

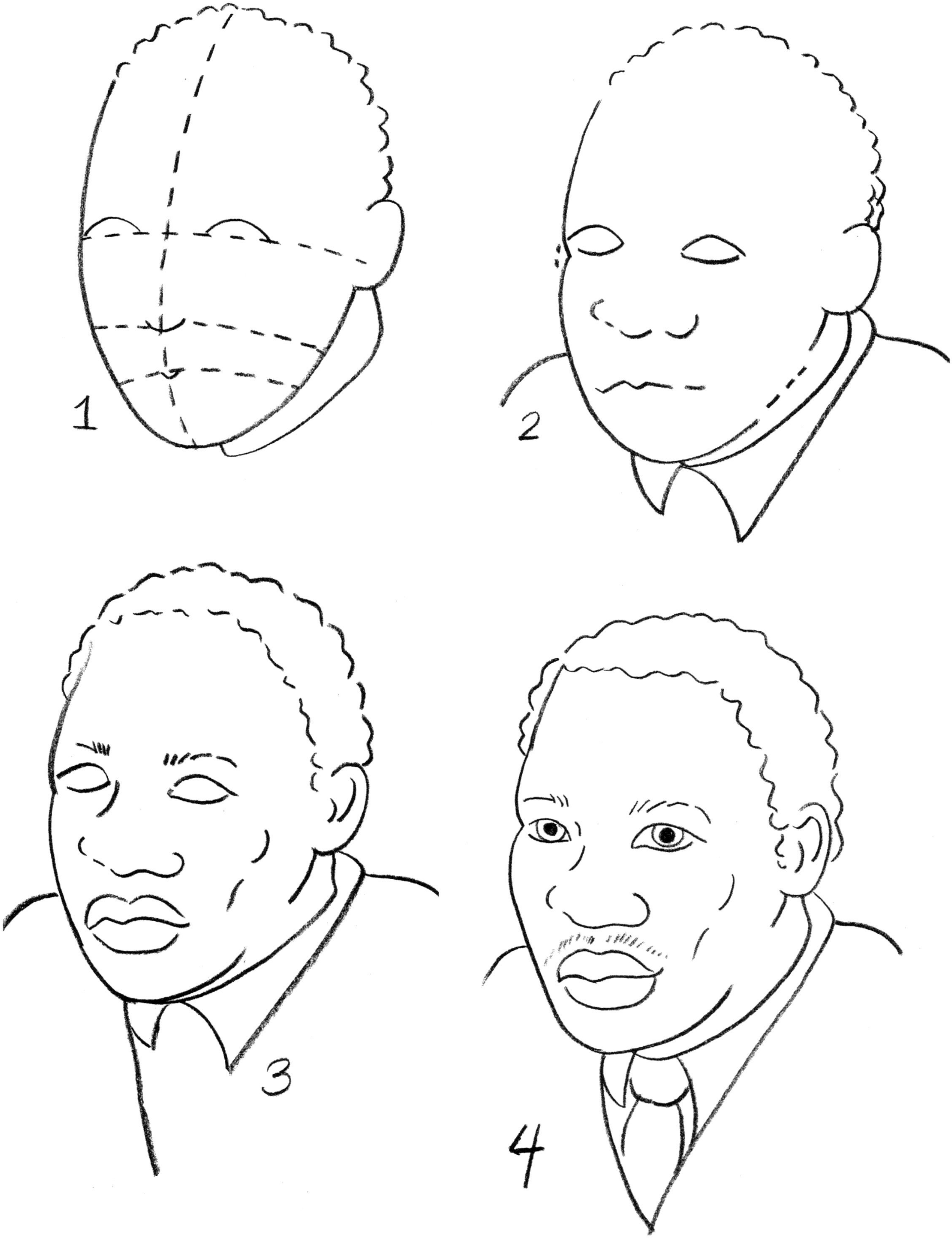
1
2
3
4

1
2
3
4

1
2
3
4
HAPPY VALENTINE'S DAY TO YOU

1
2
3

1
2
3

1
2
3
4

1
2
3
4

1
2
3
4

1
2
3
4

1
2
3
4
1
2
3
4

1

2

3

4

1
2
3
4

1
2
3
4

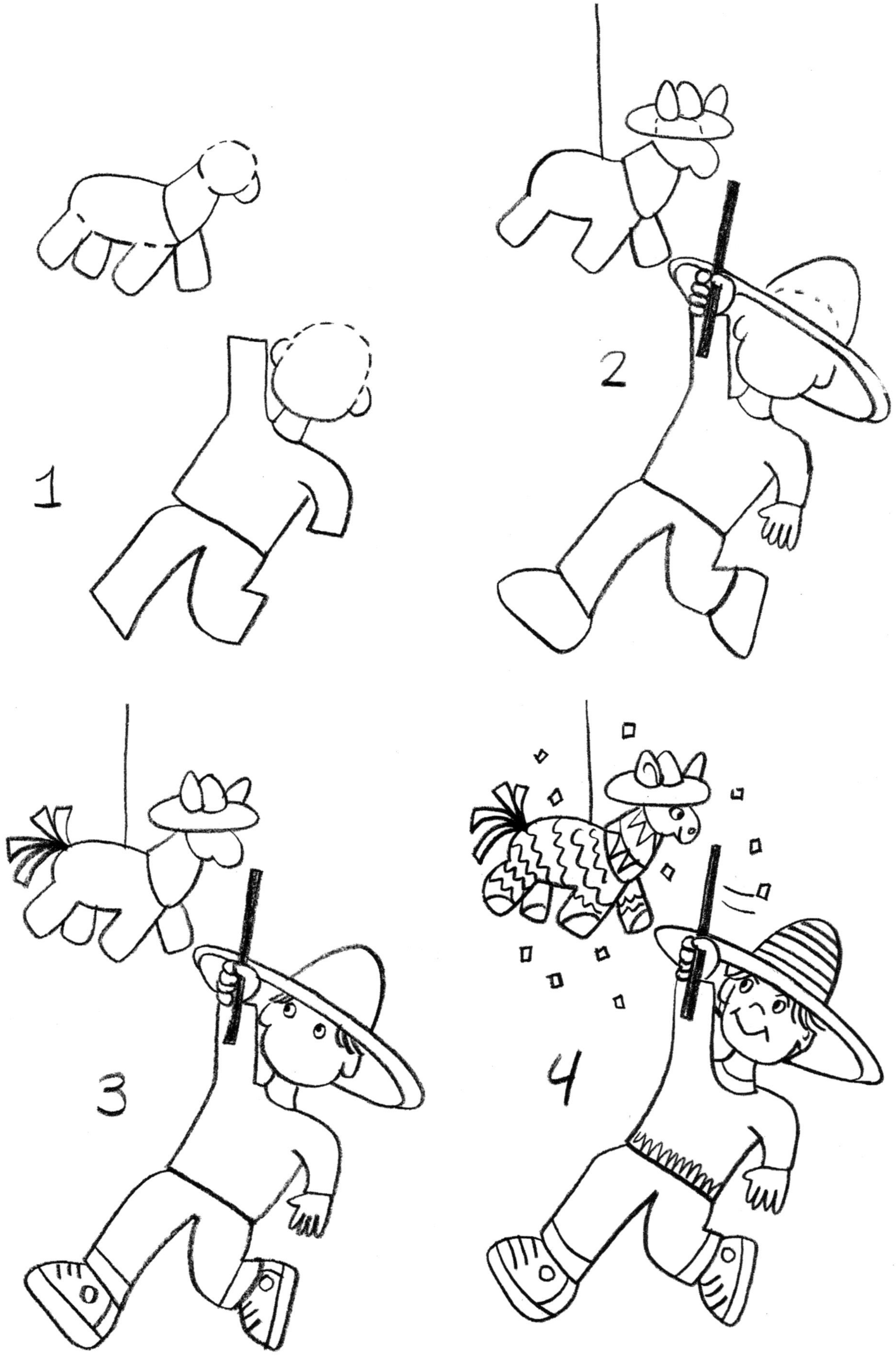
1
2
3
4

1
2
3
4

1
2
3
4

1
2
3
4

1
2
3
4
SANTA MARIA

1
2
3
4

1

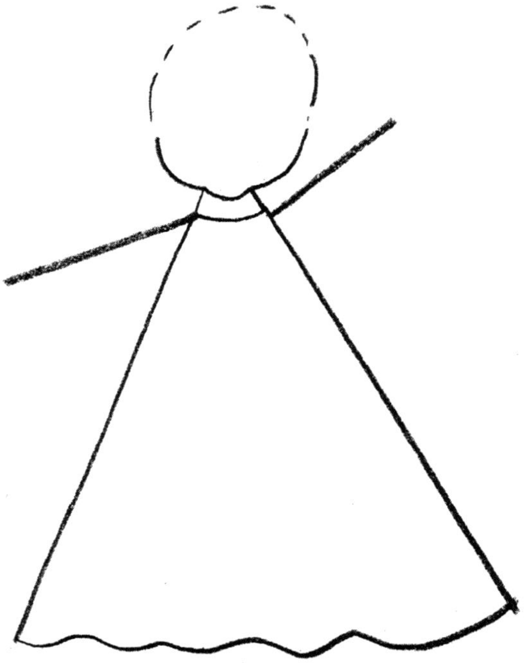

2

3

4

1
2
3
4

1
2
3
4

1

2

3

4

1
2
3
4

1
2
3
4

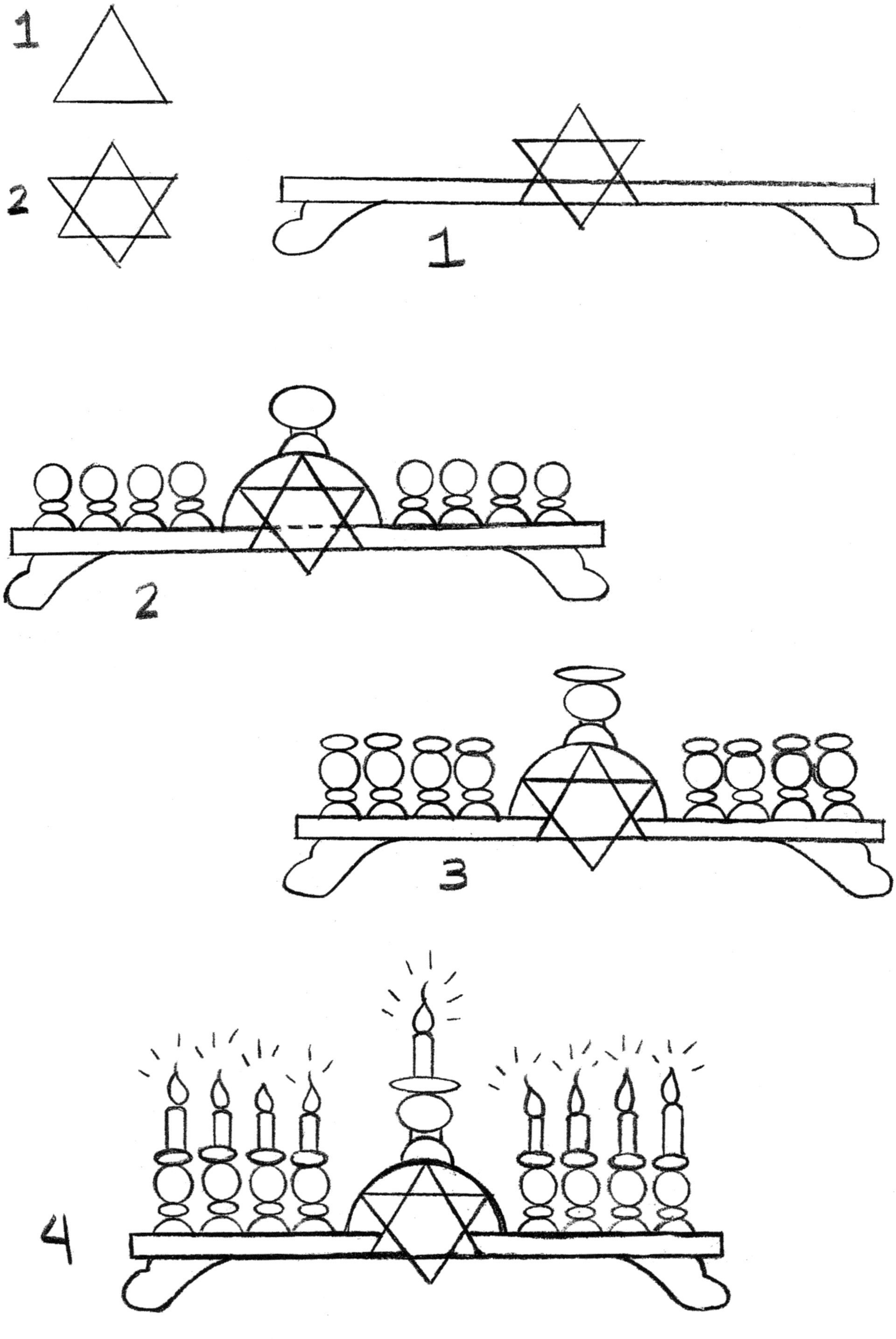
1
2
1
2
3
4

1
2
3
4
ה
נ

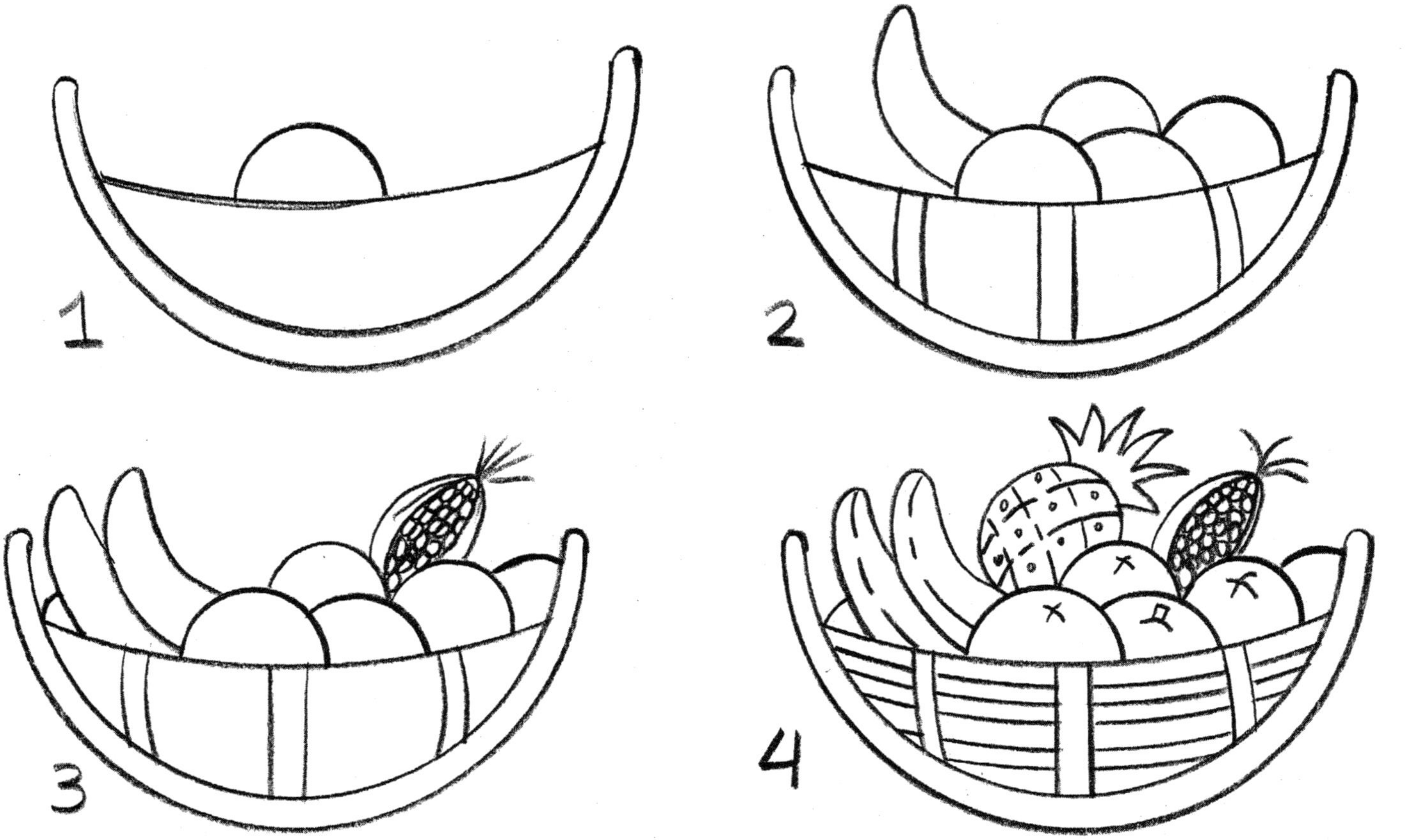
1
2
3
4

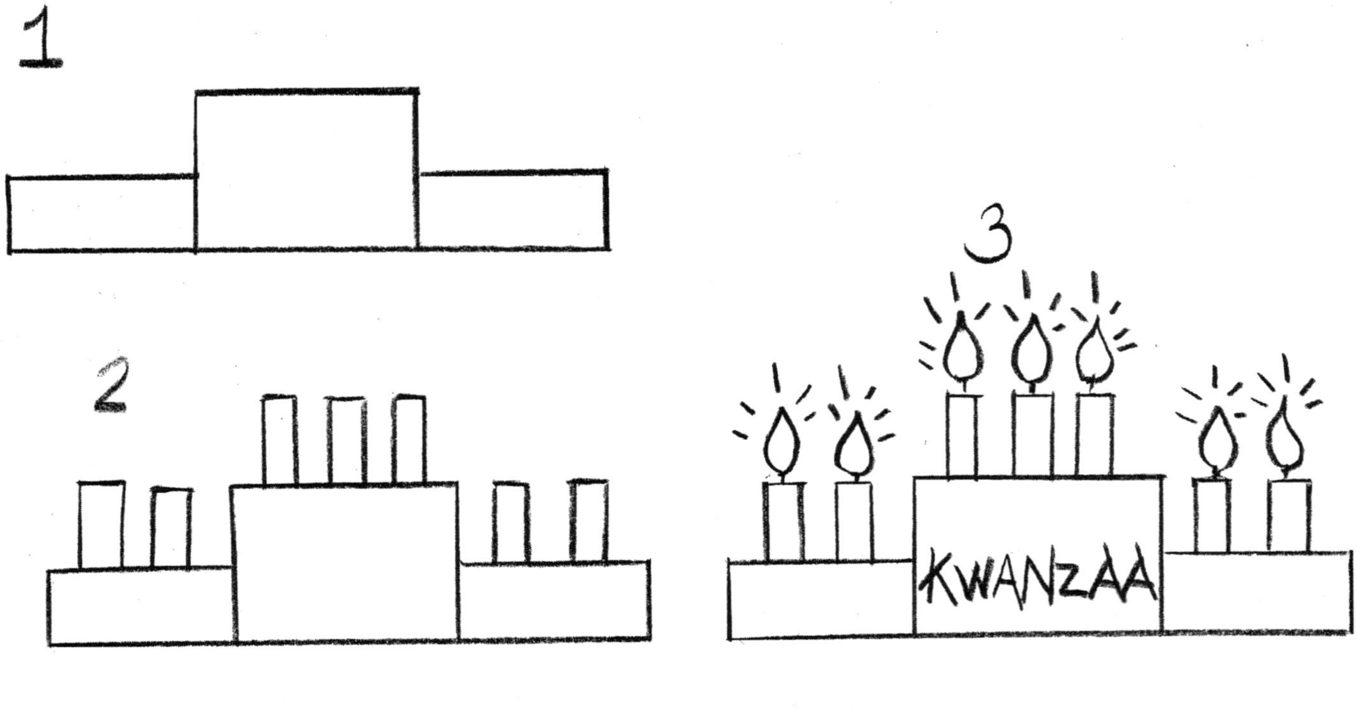
1
2
3
KWANZAA